Safety Plays in Bridge

As every expert knows, the big winners at this game are not the players capable of executing an occasional sparkling coup but those who know how to avoid defeat in everyday contracts when the breaks are bad.

Unlucky breaks can be guarded against by the use of safety plays, and here two famous authors explain, with many lively examples, the correct safety play for every combination of the cards. A study of this book is sure to result in more successes, fewer failures, and a consequent boost of confidence.

The authors have won equal distinction as players and as writers on the game. For many years Roger Trézel was an automatic choice for the French International Team, as was Terence Reese for the British. Both are European and World Champions.

Master Bridge Series
General Editor: Hugh Kelsey

A distinguished new series which contains
books by the world's foremost experts on all
aspects of the game, ranging from Hugh Kelsey's
own book for beginners to books on advanced
techniques of bidding and play.

Terence Reese and Roger Trézel

Safety Plays in Bridge

LONDON
VICTOR GOLLANCZ LTD
in association with Peter Crawley

© Terence Reese and Roger Trézel 1976

First published in 1976 by Ward Lock Limited
Second impression August 1979

ISBN 0 575 02748 7

Printed and bound by R. J. Acford Ltd,
Chichester, Sussex

Introduction

by Terence Reese

The play of the cards at bridge is a big subject, capable of filling many large books. Some years ago Roger Trézel, the great French player and writer, had the idea of breaking up the game into several books of the present length, each dealing with one of the standard forms of technique. He judged, quite rightly as it turned out, that this scheme would appeal both to comparative beginners, who would be able to learn the game by stages, and to experienced players wishing to extend their knowledge of a particular branch of play.

We have now worked together on an English version, profiting from his experience. The first four titles in the series are:

1 Safety Plays in Bridge
2 Blocking and Unblocking Plays in Bridge
3 Elimination Play in Bridge
4 Snares and Swindles in Bridge

Other titles are in preparation.

Safety Plays

Safety plays are a form of insurance against a bad break.

Suppose, for example, that a normal division of the adverse cards would enable you to lose no tricks at all in the suit that interests you, whereas against very bad distribution you might lose two tricks; if there is a way to lose just one trick, *whatever the distribution*, then a safety play is available and you must employ it whenever the contract depends on losing not more than one trick. Putting it another way, you sacrifice a trick when the distribution is favourable, but when it is unfavourable you make sure you do not lose two tricks.

It is essential to know all the standard safety plays; they will reward you many times over. The occasional overtricks you give up, worth 20 or 30 points apiece, will be amply compensated by the thousands of points you will gain by ensuring your contract.

A special point about safety plays is that it is not necessary to count the hands or to know the adverse distribution: all you need is to realize that a particular suit may break badly. It is enough, when you are playing a contract that seems to be lay-down, to pause and say to yourself: 'Can I lose this contract if the breaks are extremely bad ?' If the answer is yes, then look for a safety play that will protect you against such distribution.

Example 1

You hold between dummy and yourself eight cards of a suit including the ace, king and ten. These cards may all be in the same hand or in opposite hands. Your object is to lose not more than one trick in the suit. First lead the ace and then lead a low card, intending to put in the ten if the left-hand opponent has also played low. These are typical holdings:

K 10 x x x	K 10 x x	A K 10 x
A x x	A x x x	x x x x
A K 10 x x	K 10 8 x x x	A K 10 9 x x
x x x	A 9	x x

If the finesse of the ten loses to the jack or queen, then the distribution must be 3—2 and the remaining honour will fall under the king on the next round. Meanwhile, you insure against Q J x x on the left. If these cards are on the right, nothing can be done. Note that in the last two examples, where declarer has only a doubleton, it is necessary to add some strengthening cards; otherwise a defender with, say, Q J 9 x could render the safety play ineffective by splitting his honours on the second round.

You play the following hand as South in a contract of four hearts:

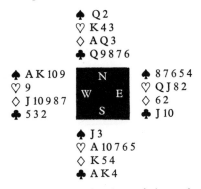

♠ Q 2
♡ K 4 3
◇ A Q 3
♣ Q 9 8 7 6

♠ A K 10 9
♡ 9
◇ J 10 9 8 7
♣ 5 3 2

♠ 8 7 6 5 4
♡ Q J 8 2
◇ 6 2
♣ J 10

♠ J 3
♡ A 10 7 6 5
◇ K 5 4
♣ A K 4

West leads the king and ace of spades, then switches to the jack of diamonds. South wins and sees that there are no more losers outside the trump suit; he must, therefore, avoid losing two trump tricks.

South leads the king of hearts from dummy, East plays the two and West the nine. On the next heart East plays the eight and now South must put in the ten. If East began with Q J 8 2, South will win this trick and lose only one heart. If East began with Q 8 2, West will capture the ten with the jack, but East's queen will fall under the ace on the next round.

Note that it would not help East, as the cards lie, to play the queen or jack on the second round. South would win, cross to dummy with a diamond or a club, and then lead up to the 10 7 6, again losing one trick. East does better not to split his honours in this type of situation; then he will make two tricks if South neglects to make the safety play.

Example 2

You hold between dummy and yourself nine cards of a suit including the ace and queen, with or without the ten, the ace and queen being in the same hand. Your object is to lose not more than one trick in the suit. You should lay down the ace, then lead up to the queen.

A Q 10 x x   x x x
x x x x   A Q x x x x

In the first example if the ace drops a singleton king from East, you lose no trick at all, as you can return to hand to finesse the ten. In the second example you lose one trick if the king is single on your left, but if you had finessed the queen you would have lost a second trick to East's J 10 x.

You play the following hand as South in a contract of six spades:

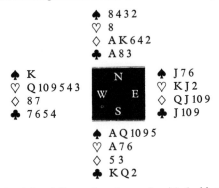

♠ 8 4 3 2
♡ 8
♢ A K 6 4 2
♣ A 8 3

♠ K
♡ Q 10 9 5 4 3
♢ 8 7
♣ 7 6 5 4

♠ J 7 6
♡ K J 2
♢ Q J 10 9
♣ J 10 9

♠ A Q 10 9 5
♡ A 7 6
♢ 5 3
♣ K Q 2

West leads the eight of diamonds and you win with the king in dummy. You see that there are no losers outside the trump suit; therefore your sole concern is to avoid losing two tricks in spades.

If you lead a spade from dummy and finesse the queen, losing to West's king, you will have to guess on the next round whether to play for the drop (by leading the ace) or to take a finesse against the jack. You would be in the same dilemma if you finessed the ten on the first round and lost to the jack: West might hold the K J or the jack might be single.

The correct play is to lay down the ace on the first round. If West follows with a low card, you re-enter dummy and lead towards the queen. If West sits over you with the K J x, there is nothing to be done, but if East has three cards, or if the distribution is 2—2, you lose just one trick.

When the king is single, as in the diagram above, you lose no tricks at all, as you can safely cross to dummy and finesse against East's J x. If West has K J alone, or the jack alone, you lose just one trick. But if you finesse the queen on the first round, losing to the king, you will have to 'take a view' on the next round, and it is even money that you will do the wrong thing.

Example 3

You hold with the dummy eight cards of a suit including the ace and queen, these two cards in the same hand. Your object is to lose *not more than two* tricks in the suit. Again, the first play should be to lay down the ace. The situation is analogous to that of the previous example, but it occurs more often. These are common holdings:

```
A Q x x      A Q x x x      A Q x x x x
x x x x      x x x          x x
```

If your play of the ace drops a singleton king, you lose only two tricks in the suit instead of three, as would happen if you took the finesse. If the king does not appear you lead low towards the queen on the next round. Note that if West holds, say, K J x, you lose nothing by refusing the finesse on the first round. Even if West holds K J 10 x, you still lose only two tricks. The difference arises when East holds a singleton king.

When South played the following hand in three no trumps, he had to take certain other factors into consideration.

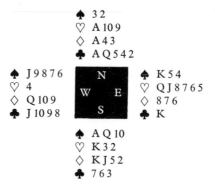

```
              ♠ 3 2
              ♡ A 10 9
              ◇ A 4 3
              ♣ A Q 5 4 2
♠ J 9 8 7 6                  ♠ K 5 4
♡ 4           N             ♡ Q J 8 7 6 5
◇ Q 10 9    W   E           ◇ 8 7 6
♣ J 10 9 8     S            ♣ K
              ♠ A Q 10
              ♡ K 3 2
              ◇ K J 5 2
              ♣ 7 6 3
```

West led the seven of spades (fourth best). East played the king and South won with the ace. (With A Q x South would have held up on the first trick, but the ten makes a big difference, as will shortly appear.) Declarer could count six certain tricks outside the clubs, so three tricks in clubs would be enough. This was clearly a moment for safety play, the more so as it would be extremely inconvenient to allow East to win and play a spade through the Q 10.

South led a club to the ace, therefore, dropping the singleton king.
Very lucky, you may think. But there was more to the play than just the
chance of catching the king. When South led the club from hand he had
these possibilities in mind:

1) If West played the king, he would be allowed to hold the trick and
would not be able to attack spades except by leading up to the Q 10.
2) If West played low, and East also played low on the ace, declarer
intended to return a club from dummy. West might have J x, and when
in with the jack he would be unable to do any damage.
3) Better still, East might hold K x; in that case the clubs would be
established for the loss of one trick.
4) Finally, West might hold K J 10 9, but even then he could be held to
two tricks in clubs.

After the ace of clubs had dropped the king, South returned a club from
dummy. West took his only chance now by leading the jack of spades.
He hoped that either South held A Q x, in which case his partner
would unblock by playing the ten under the jack, or that South held A Q x x,
in which case East's ten would fall, and the queen could be forced out.
But West was out of luck. South captured the jack of spades with the
queen, gave up a club to establish the suit, and ended up with ten tricks—
three spades, three clubs, and four top cards in the red suits.

There is one further point worth noting about the type of safety plays we
have been discussing in this section. The same effect may be obtained by
ducking the first round of the suit instead of playing the ace. If the king is
single, it will beat the air—which is better than letting it capture the queen.
On many hands it is safer to duck the first round than to play the ace.
Suppose the trump suit is distributed in this way:

$$\begin{array}{ccc} & \text{x x x} & \\ \text{K J 10 x} & & \text{x} \\ & \text{A Q x x x} & \end{array}$$

To lay down the ace and later lead up to the queen gives up all control.
The declarer will probably be better placed if he ducks the first round and
goes up with the ace when East shows out on the second round.

Example 4

You hold with the dummy nine cards of a suit, including the ace, king and queen, but not the ten or jack. Your object is to lose no trick in the suit.

```
A x x          K 8 x x        K Q 8 x x
K Q 9 x x x    A Q 9 x x      A 9 x x
```

In each case it is correct to begin with the high card that is on its own— the ace in the first example.

One of the present authors had a bitter experience when the following hand occurred at rubber bridge:

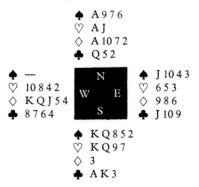

```
                    ♠ A 9 7 6
                    ♡ A J
                    ◇ A 10 7 2
                    ♣ Q 5 2
        ♠ —                        ♠ J 10 4 3
        ♡ 10 8 4 2      N          ♡ 6 5 3
        ◇ K Q J 5 4   W   E        ◇ 9 8 6
        ♣ 8 7 6 4       S          ♣ J 10 9
                    ♠ K Q 8 5 2
                    ♡ K Q 9 7
                    ◇ 3
                    ♣ A K 3
```

North, the dealer, had agreed to play a strong no trump of 16—18 points, but facing an inexperienced partner he decided to open one no trump rather than one spade. He was a point short for the bid, but hoped to play the hand. Alas! South forced with three spades, followed with a Blackwood four no trumps on the next round, and then propelled himself into seven spades!

West led the king of diamonds, and after putting down his dummy North glimpsed the J 10 4 3 of spades in the East hand. To his horror, he saw his partner begin with a low spade to the king. From that moment it was all over.

South was quite a talented player, but he had not learned his safety plays. The only danger was a 4—0 break in trumps. If West held the four trumps, there would be no way to pick them up without loss. But if East held them, the play of the ace from dummy would disclose the void and there would be no problem then in picking up the J 10 x. On the next round East would play the ten and South the king; then declarer would cross to dummy and finesse against East's J 4.

North was left with the ironical reflection that if he had opened one spade instead of one no trump he would have played the slam contract himself!

Example 5

You hold in dummy and your own hand ten cards of a suit, missing the king and ten. The queen and jack are in different hands and your object is to lose no trick.

Jxxxxx	Jxxx	Q98xx
AQ9x	AQ9xxx	AJxxx

You should lead first the single honour—the jack in the first two examples, the queen in the third.

Suppose that the player who bid the last hand with such fire were to play the following hand in seven hearts:

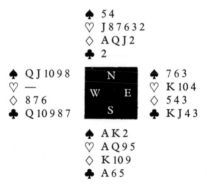

```
                    ♠ 5 4
                    ♡ J 8 7 6 3 2
                    ◇ A Q J 2
                    ♣ 2
   ♠ Q J 10 9 8        N          ♠ 7 6 3
   ♡ —            W         E     ♡ K 10 4
   ◇ 8 7 6                        ◇ 5 4 3
   ♣ Q 10 9 8 7        S          ♣ K J 4 3
                    ♠ A K 2
                    ♡ A Q 9 5
                    ◇ K 10 9
                    ♣ A 6 5
```

West leads the queen of spades and South wins with the ace.
He has three possible ways of entering dummy for a heart finesse: he can ruff the third round of spades, cross to the queen of diamonds, or ruff the second round of clubs. The club ruff, if there has been no adverse bidding, is the safest of these, so South cashes the ace of clubs, ruffs a club, and leads a low heart from the table. East plays the four and South, after deep reflection, the queen.

Now he must lose a trick to the king of hearts. One can imagine the post-mortem.

South: 'Sorry, partner. I suppose I overbid, but we might have been luckier.'

Seeing that North is shaking his head, South goes on:

'I took the best chance, didn't I ? I mean, it wouldn't be right to put in the nine, would it ? Or to play for the drop of a singleton king ?'

North: 'No, you can't play for the drop with ten cards—that would be well against the odds. But if you are going to finesse, you must lead the *jack* from dummy on the first round. If East holds K x, it makes no difference whether you lead the jack or a small card. But when East has K 10 x, as on this occasion, leading the jack solves all your problems. If East plays low, you let the jack run, of course. If he covers, then West's void is shown up and all you have to do is enter dummy again for a finesse against the 10 x. Not very difficult!'

Example 6

You and dummy hold nine cards of a suit, missing K 10 9 x. The queen and jack are in separate hands and your object is to lose not more than one trick.

| J x x x | J 8 7 x x | Q x x |
| A Q 8 x x | A Q x x | A J 8 x x x |

As in the previous set of examples, you must begin with the single honour—the jack in the first two examples, the queen in the third.

Suppose you play the following hand in a contract of six clubs:

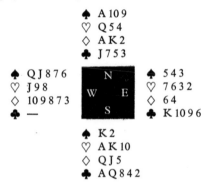

```
                    ♠ A 10 9
                    ♡ Q 5 4
                    ◇ A K 2
                    ♣ J 7 5 3
    ♠ Q J 8 7 6              ♠ 5 4 3
    ♡ J 9 8          N        ♡ 7 6 3 2
    ◇ 10 9 8 7 3   W   E     ◇ 6 4
    ♣ —              S        ♣ K 10 9 6
                    ♠ K 2
                    ♡ A K 10
                    ◇ Q J 5
                    ♣ A Q 8 4 2
```

West leads the queen of spades and you win with the ace in dummy. There are no losers outside the trump suit, so all that concerns you is not to lose two club tricks.

If the clubs are 3—1 or 2—2, you will never lose more than one trick. (It is true that you might finesse and then sustain an unlucky ruff. If you held the nine or ten of clubs in addition, you would play the ace first for that reason, but in the present case you have to consider the more likely possibility of a defender holding K 10 9 x.) Suppose, then, that all four clubs are in one hand. If West holds them, you cannot avoid losing two tricks. You concentrate, therefore, on the possibility of East holding K 10 9 x.

Employing the same technique as in the previous examples, you lead the *jack* from dummy. East will probably cover with the king. You win with the ace and return a low club to the seven. East can win this trick but his last two clubs will be exposed to a finesse.

The same style of play is followed when you are missing A 10 9 x, as in these situations:

$$Q 7 5 4 3 \qquad K Q 6 5 2$$
$$K J 8 2 \qquad J 8 7 3$$

In the first example you lead the queen from dummy, so that you will be able to pick up A 10 9 x in the East hand. In the second example you lead the jack from hand, so that you can pick up West's A 10 9 x. You can achieve the same effect, it is true, by leading a low card away from the hand containing the two honours. The mistake would be to play one of the double honours on the first round, because then you would lose two tricks whenever the suit was divided 4—0.

Example 7

We move now to a different type of safety play, where the way to make sure of the critical trick is to take a deep finesse. The commonest example occurs when declarer has nine cards of a suit missing Q J x x.

K 10 x x   A 10 x
A 9 x x x   K 9 x x x x

Suppose that you can afford to lose one trick, but in no circumstances two tricks. You must not lead one of the high honours, nor must you lead a low card and play an honour when the second hand has played low. Instead, you must lead low and simply cover the card played by the next player. Say that in the first example you lead low towards the dummy and West plays low; you put in the ten, and if this loses to the jack or queen the remaining cards of the suit must fall under the ace and king. If, instead, you play the king from dummy, and East shows void, you will lose two tricks to West.

An example of this safety play occurred during a match between France and Belgium in the European Championship.

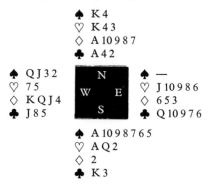

West felt very happy when his opponents reached a contract of six spades. He had an excellent lead in the king of diamonds and a very promising holding in the trump suit.

But his hopes were quickly shattered. Declarer won the first trick with the ace of diamonds, led a club to the king, and the five of spades from hand. West, of course, played low, but to his dismay South let the five run. After that, he lost just one trump trick.

No need to suppose that West was holding his cards in the middle of the table! The finesse of the five was eminently correct, because the only danger to the hand was that West, having followed to the first round, might hold all the outstanding trumps.

Note that this deep finesse with nine cards missing the queen and jack is a 'perfect' safety play, providing complete insurance against the loss of two tricks.

Example 8

You hold eight cards of a suit, with the A K 8 in one hand, the 10 in
other. The object, again, is to lose at most one trick.

$$10 \, x \, x \, x \qquad 10 \, x \, x$$
$$A \, K \, 8 \, x \qquad A \, K \, 8 \, x \, x$$

You should begin by laying down the ace. Now, if the queen or jack
or nine appears on your left, the queen or jack on your right, you follow with
a low card from hand towards the 10 x x. This play saves you from losing
two tricks when West has a singleton queen, jack or nine, and when East
has a singleton queen or jack. It is true that in some cases, after the queen
or jack has fallen, you will miss the chance to drop a doubleton QJ, losing
no tricks at all; but your aim, remember, is to lose at most one trick.

Here is a typical situation in a slam contract:

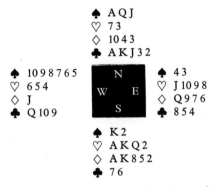

```
              ♠ A Q J
              ♡ 7 3
              ◇ 10 4 3
              ♣ A K J 3 2
  ♠ 10 9 8 7 6 5              ♠ 4 3
  ♡ 6 5 4                     ♡ J 10 9 8
  ◇ J                         ◇ Q 9 7 6
  ♣ Q 10 9                    ♣ 8 5 4
              ♠ K 2
              ♡ A K Q 2
              ◇ A K 8 5 2
              ♣ 7 6
```

South played in six no trumps and the ten of spades was led. Four tricks
in diamonds or four tricks in club would be enough for the slam, and it was
natural to play on diamonds first because this was by far the stronger
suit. The declarer, therefore, began with a low diamond towards the ace,
on which the jack appeared from West.

South might have gone for an overtrick now by playing off the king of
diamonds. Even if the queen did not fall, he would have chances to
establish sufficient tricks in clubs. But there was a much safer line: a low
diamond from hand could not fail to establish four tricks in the suit. The
ten lost to the queen, but South then held K 8 5 over East's 9 7.

Declarer would have made the same play of a low diamond after the ace
if the honour card had fallen from East, and also if West had produced the
nine; this might be from J 9 or Q 9, but if the nine were single it would
be a calamitous error to play off the king.

The safety play described in this section is clearly not 'perfect'. It will not
succeed if either defender holds Q J 9 x (not to mention Q J 9 x x).
Furthermore if it were East who held Q J 9 x, a different line of play would
be more successful. But as a safety play it is still valid, because it is more
likely than any other line of play to keep the losers to one.

Example 9

You and dummy hold eight or nine cards between you, missing the queen and ten. The ace and king are in different hands. Your object, as usual, is to lose not more than one trick.

K 9 x	A J x x	K J x x
A J x x x	K 9 x x x	A 9 x x

In each case you should begin with the high card in the hand that contains the jack. On the next round, if your opponent plays low, you put in the nin This line of play is proof against Q 10 x x in either defending hand.

You play the following hand in a contract of four spades:

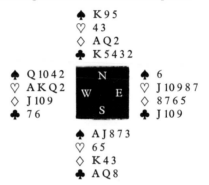

♠ K 9 5
♡ 4 3
◇ A Q 2
♣ K 5 4 3 2

♠ Q 10 4 2
♡ A K Q 2
◇ J 10 9
♣ 7 6

♠ 6
♡ J 10 9 8 7
◇ 8 7 6 5
♣ J 10 9

♠ A J 8 7 3
♡ 6 5
◇ K 4 3
♣ A Q 8

West begins with the king and ace of hearts, then switches to the jack of diamonds. Your only concern now is not to lose two tricks in the trump suit. You can readily afford to lose one trick, because you are 'solid' outside.

It would be a bad mistake in the circumstances to lay down the king of spades, intending to finesse the jack on the next round. That would be correct only if you needed to make all the tricks in spades.

Since you can afford to lose one trick, you adopt the regulation safety play. You lay down the ace of spades first, then lead low towards the K 9. If West showed out at this point you would go up with the king, of course. On the present occasion West plays low, whereupon you take the deep finesse of the nine. You do not mind if this loses to the queen or ten, because you will not be losing any more tricks.

This safety play is particularly valuable because, as was said at the beginning, it is proof against any 4—1 division; equally, of course, against any 4—0 division when you hold nine cards in the two hands.

Example 10

We turn next to a very simple, very common, combination of cards that is nevertheless a blind spot for more than half the bridge-playing world. You hold seven cards of a suit, including ace, king and jack, divided 4—3. Your object is to make three of the four possible tricks.

$$\text{A K J x} \qquad \text{A J x x} \qquad \text{A x x}$$
$$\text{x x x} \qquad \text{K x x} \qquad \text{K J x x}$$

You may think that the best chance is to cash one of the top cards, then finesse the jack, hoping either that the finesse will hold or that the suit will be divided 3—3. But that play fails when the finesse of the jack loses to a doubleton queen. The play that gives the maximum chance for three tricks is to cash both ace and king, then lead up to the J x. You win three tricks now whenever the queen is on the right side (under the jack), or the suit is divided 3—3, or *when there is a doubleton Q x over the jack.*

Most tournament players know this safety play in theory, but when the opportunity for it occurred on the following deal from a pairs contest, half the field pursued the wrong line.

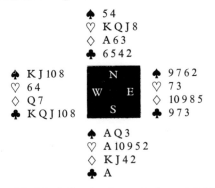

```
              ♠ 5 4
              ♡ K Q J 8
              ◇ A 6 3
              ♣ 6 5 4 2
♠ K J 10 8                    ♠ 9 7 6 2
♡ 6 4          N             ♡ 7 3
◇ Q 7       W     E          ◇ 10 9 8 5
♣ K Q J 10 8     S           ♣ 9 7 3
              ♠ A Q 3
              ♡ A 10 9 5 2
              ◇ K J 4 2
              ♣ A
```

The majority of the North-South pairs reached a contract of six hearts. West led the king of clubs, won by declarer's ace. All followed to two rounds of trumps.

Several players now saw the problem as 'one out of two finesses'. That is to say, they needed to find either the diamond finesse or the spade finesse, which as racing men know is a 3 to 1 on chance. It was natural to take the diamond finesse first, because if East held Q x x, South would be able to discard a spade from dummy on the thirteenth diamond and make thirteen tricks without risking the spade finesse.

This line of play proved to be ill-starred. West captured the jack of diamonds with the queen and returned a club. Sooner or later the spade finesse had to be taken, and this lost also.

The declarer who played in this fashion could claim that they were taking the best chance of making seven, but there was a better play for six. Since, after the trumps have broken 2—2, a spade discard from dummy will mean no losers in that suit, South should make the safety play in diamonds by leading king, then low to the ace. If the queen has not appeared, he leads a third round up to the J x, establishing a discard whenever East holds the queen. As the cards lie the queen appears on the second round of the suit and declarer later takes the spade finesse to try for an overtrick.

Readers who have some experience of tournament play will know that in a pairs event it is sometimes justifiable to take a slight risk in the hope of making extra tricks. Players who finessed the jack of diamonds on the present hand were quick to advance that argument. They were wrong, because six hearts is not all that easy a contract to reach; there were sure to be some pairs who would stay short of the slam. That being so, it was sensible to play six hearts as safely as possible, just as one would at rubber bridge.

Example 11

You hold nine cards of a suit, with the Q J in one hand, the A 9 in the other.

QJxx   A9x
A9xxx   QJxxxx

The play with these combinations, when you can afford to lose one trick, is unexpected. The only safe play is to lead a low card away from the A 9 up to the hand containing the Q J. This is safe against K 10 8 x on either side. It is therefore a 'perfect' safety play. The problem was high-lighted on this deal from a multiple team event:

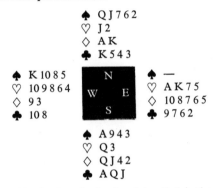

```
              ♠ Q J 7 6 2
              ♡ J 2
              ◇ A K
              ♣ K 5 4 3
♠ K 10 8 5         N          ♠ —
♡ 10 9 8 6 4   W     E        ♡ A K 7 5
◇ 9 3                         ◇ 10 8 7 6 5
♣ 10 8             S          ♣ 9 7 6 2
              ♠ A 9 4 3
              ♡ Q 3
              ◇ Q J 4 2
              ♣ A Q J
```

There was some 'duplication of values', as it is called, in the North-South hands, and some pairs got too high, playing in five or even six spades. There were also casualties among those who managed to stop in four spades!

The defence usually began with two tricks in hearts, followed by a diamond to dummy's king. Now in a pairs event, where overtricks are not to be spurned, it would be forgiveable to lead the queen of spades from dummy, losing no tricks in the suit when East held K x or K x x. But in any other form of scoring the correct line is to enter hand with a club and lead a low spade towards the dummy. This way, West makes only one trick with his K 10 8 5, whereas, if declarer begins with the queen from dummy, he must lose two tricks.

Now suppose that the K 10 8 5 had been held by East. West's void would have shown up on the first round and it would have been easy, after losing the first trick, to pick up the rest of the suit. Note, however, that when East has K 10 8 x it is fatal to begin with the ace.

Finally, it is *not* safe to lead low from dummy and put in the nine if East follows with a low card. Playing that way you lose two tricks foolishly when West holds the singleton 10 or K 10 x.

Example 12

You hold ten cards of a suit, including ace, queen and ten. The ace and the queen are in opposite hands. Your object is to lose not more than one trick.

    A 10 x x   Q 10 9 x   Q x x x x
    Q x x x x x   A x x x x x   A 10 x x x

You must on no account play off the ace. Instead, you lead towards the ace, intending to put in the ten if the next opponent plays low; or, if you are in the hand that contains the ace, you may lead low away from this card.

Suppose you reach a contract of six hearts on the following hand:

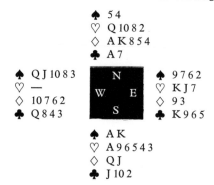

	♠ 5 4	
	♡ Q 10 8 2	
	◇ A K 8 5 4	
	♣ A 7	

♠ Q J 10 8 3   ♠ 9 7 6 2
♡ —   ♡ K J 7
◇ 10 7 6 2   ◇ 9 3
♣ Q 8 4 3   ♣ K 9 6 5

    ♠ A K
    ♡ A 9 6 5 4 3
    ◇ Q J
    ♣ J 10 2

West leads the queen of spades, which is a little lucky for you. Had the opening lead been a club, you would have had to win with the ace and play a heart to the ace, hoping either to drop the king single or to dispose of your club losers on dummy's diamonds. As it is, you have a respite. You can afford now to lose a trump trick.

If you were on the table, you would lead a low heart, intending to cover whatever card was played by East. However, it is not convenient to enter dummy and your safest play is to lead a low heart from hand. When West shows void you put in the ten, which loses to the jack. Even if East switches to a club at this point you are in no difficulty. You win in dummy, pick up the king of hearts by a finesse, and cash the Q J of diamonds. Then you cross to dummy's fourth heart and discard two clubs on the A K of diamonds.

It is easy to see that if you had led the ace of hearts from hand you would have lost two tricks to East's K J x. The other trap with this holding is to lead the queen from dummy; then you lose two tricks when East is void and West has K J x.

Example 13

You hold nine cards in the two hands, missing Q J 10 x. The ace and king are in the same hand and your object is to lose not more than one trick.

```
AK98      AK7       6543
76543     986532    AK987
```

You lead low towards the hand containing the A K, and if second hand plays low you take a deep finesse. This way, you lose only one trick when the player under the A K holds Q J 10 x.

When the following hand was played in six diamonds there was a slight variation from the examples above, in that the missing cards were Q J 9 x.

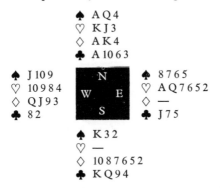

```
                    ♠ A Q 4
                    ♡ K J 3
                    ◇ A K 4
                    ♣ A 10 6 3

    ♠ J 10 9         N          ♠ 8 7 6 5
    ♡ 10 9 8 4                  ♡ A Q 7 6 5 2
    ◇ Q J 9 3    W      E       ◇ —
    ♣ 8 2            S          ♣ J 7 5

                    ♠ K 3 2
                    ♡ —
                    ◇ 10 8 7 6 5 2
                    ♣ K Q 9 4
```

North, holding a balanced 21 points, opened two no trumps and South responded three diamonds. North bid three spades to show that the diamond response interested him, and eventually six diamonds was reached.

West led the ten of hearts, the jack was covered by the queen, and South ruffed with the five. He then led the two of diamonds and West played the three (it would have been a bad mistake to put in the nine). South played the king from dummy and thereafter had to lose two trump tricks.

South was an experienced player and knew quite well that he had carelessly omitted to make the safe (and artistic) play of finessing the four of trumps on the first round. If he lost the trick to East, obviously the rest of the diamonds would fall under the A K.

The only excuse that South could offer was that there might have been a loser in clubs, and that therefore it might have been unwise to make an exaggerated play in diamonds. But this was a feeble defence, for he would not need to tackle clubs until the end of the play, and by that time it would be easy to judge which, if either, defender might hold J x x x of this suit.

Example 14

You hold eight cards of a suit, with the A Q J all in the same hand.
Your object, as in most safety plays, is to lose not more than one trick in
the suit.

$$
\begin{array}{cc}
\text{A Q J x x} & \text{A Q J x} \\
\text{x x x} & \text{x x x x}
\end{array}
$$

The best play, assuming that sufficient entries are available to the hand
opposite the A Q J, is to lay down the ace first and subsequently to lead
towards the Q J x. This play saves a trick when there is a singleton king
over the A Q J and it never costs; at least, it never costs the vital trick.
The play is similar to Example 2, where, it will be recalled, it was right to
play the ace first with A Q x x x opposite x x x.

South played the following hand in six no trumps:

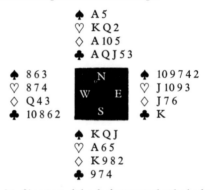

```
                    ♠ A 5
                    ♡ K Q 2
                    ◇ A 10 5
                    ♣ A Q J 5 3
    ♠ 8 6 3          N         ♠ 10 9 7 4 2
    ♡ 8 7 4      W       E     ♡ J 10 9 3
    ◇ Q 4 3          S         ◇ J 7 6
    ♣ 10 8 6 2                 ♣ K
                    ♠ K Q J
                    ♡ A 6 5
                    ◇ K 9 8 2
                    ♣ 9 7 4
```

West led the eight of hearts and the declarer saw that he had eight top
tricks outside the club suit. As in some circumstances it might be
necessary to preserve the entries to his own hand, he won the first trick in
dummy, then played off the ace of clubs. When this dropped the king he
gave up a trick in clubs and made the slam.

Was this just a lucky view? Not at all! South was making a regulation
safety play to guard against a singleton king. As the cards lie, it would have
been fatal to take a finesse, as West would still have had a guard in clubs.

Now suppose that East had held a low singleton in clubs and West had held
K 10 8 x. After cashing the ace of clubs, South would come to hand with
the king of diamonds to lead a second club towards the Q J x x. West
plays low (best). Declarer then crosses to the ace of hearts to play another
club, establishing two more tricks in the suit. He makes as many tricks as
if he had taken the finesse. Playing off the ace loses a trick when West
holds K x or K x x, but that, on the present hand, would not be a vital trick.

Example 15

One important form of safety play consists of protecting a winner from
an adverse ruff. When the card in question will be equally useful later in the
play, it may be wise not to play it until trumps have been drawn. That was
the situation when the following hand was played:

♠ A 6 4 3
♡ K 5
♢ A Q 8
♣ A K 7 3

♠ 8
♡ A 4 3
♢ K J 10 9 7 2
♣ J 4 2

North-South were vulnerable and West, the dealer, opened four spades.
North doubled and East passed. Good players do not double on the strength
of trump tricks alone, so South decided to play for a vulnerable game with
a bid of five diamonds. This suited North very well, and he raised to
six diamonds.

When West led the king of spades and the dummy went down, South
reached for the ace of spades—then quickly drew his hand back. The ace of
spades might be ruffed and then there would probably be a loser in clubs
as well. Having reflected on this, the declarer played low from dummy.
East, in fact, was void of spades and held four clubs to the queen, so it
would have been fatal to play the ace of spades. When West followed with
another high spade, South ruffed in hand, drew two rounds of trumps, then
took his heart ruff. He returned to hand with another spade ruff to draw the
last trump, and the ace of spades later supplied a discard for his losing club.

The play of ducking the first spade was not too difficult here, because
of West's four-spade opening. But players do not always advertise their
long suits, and a great many contracts can be saved by refusing to allow
a winning card to be ruffed.

Examples 16 and 17

When one holds touching cards, such as K Q or J 10, and wishes to force out opposing winners, there is a natural tendency to begin the assault with one of these cards. It is a temptation that must be resisted, for unless you have a powerful sequence of touching cards it is often better to lead low on the first round. Here is a typical hand to illustrate the point:

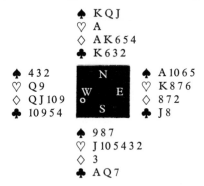

```
              ♠ K Q J
              ♡ A
              ◇ A K 6 5 4
              ♣ K 6 3 2

  ♠ 4 3 2         N        ♠ A 10 6 5
  ♡ Q 9                    ♡ K 8 7 6
  ◇ Q J 10 9   W     E     ◇ 8 7 2
  ♣ 10 9 5 4       S       ♣ J 8

              ♠ 9 8 7
              ♡ J 10 5 4 3 2
              ◇ 3
              ♣ A Q 7
```

After you have rebid your modest hearts, your partner has unselfishly raised you to game in the suit. West leads the queen of diamonds and you see at once that, with one side loser in spades, you have to avoid losing three tricks in the trump suit.

You win the first trick with the ace of diamonds, cash the ace of hearts, and come to hand with the ace of clubs. The fate of the contract depends on which heart you play next. If you lead the jack or ten, West will win with the queen and you will lose two more tricks eventually to the K 8. Clearly a low heart works better, for then you retain the J 10 as equals against the king.

When a mistake of this kind is pointed out, the declarer is apt to say, 'But if I lead low I risk giving them a cheap trick with the eight or some such card.' That is an illusion. If the hearts are 3—3, South will be able to lead the suit a third time and knock the honours together, so it makes no difference whether he leads high or low on the second round. If a defender holds K Q 9 x, he will make three tricks anyway. It can *never* gain to lead the jack or ten on the second round.

Here is another deal that exhibits the same principle:

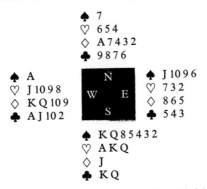

```
              ♠ 7
              ♡ 6 5 4
              ◇ A 7 4 3 2
              ♣ 9 8 7 6
 ♠ A                      ♠ J 10 9 6
 ♡ J 10 9 8      N        ♡ 7 3 2
 ◇ K Q 10 9   W     E     ◇ 8 6 5
 ♣ A J 10 2      S        ♣ 5 4 3
              ♠ K Q 8 5 4 3 2
              ♡ A K Q
              ◇ J
              ♣ K Q
```

South opened two spades, forcing for one round, and finished in four spades. West led the king of diamonds, won by dummy's ace. On the seven of spades East played the ten, quite a wily card.

South might have played East for A 10 alone, but he knew his safety plays and had the self-discipline to play low from hand. West's ace now captured nothing of value and the defence made just one more trump and the ace of clubs.

A little experimenting will show that when the object is to lose not more than two tricks with this combination, to play the king or queen on the first round cannot gain. If East had held, say, A J 10, he would have made a trick with the ten and later a trick with the ace—exactly the same as if South had played the king on the ten and returned a low one.

33

Example 18

It quite often happens that a relatively low card, such as the nine, will help to establish tricks in a suit even when the opposite hand contains the A K Q 10.

A declarer at rubber bridge found a way to go down in three no trumps on the deal below. No abstruse safety play was required; all that was needed was to count the tricks and, as it were, make use of all the troops available.

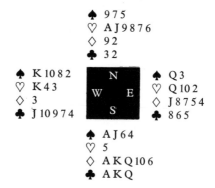

```
              ♠ 9 7 5
              ♡ A J 9 8 7 6
              ◇ 9 2
              ♣ 3 2
 ♠ K 10 8 2      N        ♠ Q 3
 ♡ K 4 3    W        E    ♡ Q 10 2
 ◇ 3             S        ◇ J 8 7 5 4
 ♣ J 10 9 7 4             ♣ 8 6 5
              ♠ A J 6 4
              ♡ 5
              ◇ A K Q 10 6
              ♣ A K Q
```

South opened with a conventional two clubs and North responded two hearts, which in the system showed simply the ace of hearts. South bid three diamonds and North three hearts. Now South sensibly bid three no trumps; had he chosen three spades, the partnership would have gone past the best contract.

West led the jack of clubs against three no trumps, and South's opening manoeuvre was to lay down the ace and king of diamonds. Goodbye to the game! East now had a double stop in diamonds and the declarer was held to eight tricks.

It is easy to see that South could have ensured four tricks in diamonds by giving up a trick to the jack. He can play off the ace of diamonds first, because the jack might be single; when this card does not appear, he should follow with a low diamond to the nine.

There are many similar situations where the safest way to establish an extra trick is to make full use of the low cards. For example:

          1) 9 8   2) 10 3
             K Q J 4 2   A K Q 8 5 2

With the cards in the first diagram, South can make sure of three tricks by running the eight. If he makes the normal play of leading up to the K Q J 6 4 and playing an honour, he will make only two tricks when either defender holds A 10 7 x x, or when West holds the singleton ace. In the second example low from hand ensures five tricks against J 9 x x x on either side.

Example 19

Many forms of safety play are easy to execute so long as you know the type and are on your guard. But when you meet them for the first time in your career you may go wrong if you have not been warned. One of the authors misplayed the following hand in his youth, but has not made the same mistake since!

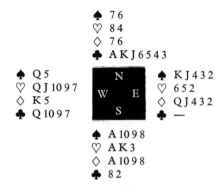

The contract was three no trumps and West led the queen of hearts. South won and led a low club, on which West inserted the ten and dummy the jack. East showed out and South suddenly found himself making just three tricks in clubs instead of six. He went two down in the vulnerable game instead of making an overtrick.

The safe play, of course, was to duck in dummy on the first round of clubs. If East follows suit, the rest of the clubs must be good, and if East shows void, it is simple to take a finesse later against West's guarded queen. The club situation on this deal gives rise to a very pretty deceptive play. Suppose West, on the first round of clubs, puts in the *queen*! Then it would take a very careful player indeed in the South chair not to cover with the king.

Example 20

In the safety plays that have been discussed so far we have always
assumed that the declarer has no entry problems and that he can go freely
from hand to hand to make the necessary leads. At the table it is often not
like that at all. The essence of many safety plays is that the declarer
foresees an entry problem and sacrifices a possible trick to overcome it.

As South, you play the following hand in three no trumps:

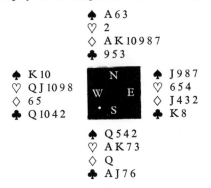

```
                ♠ A 6 3
                ♡ 2
                ◇ A K 10 9 8 7
                ♣ 9 5 3
  ♠ K 10              N           ♠ J 9 8 7
  ♡ Q J 10 9 8                    ♡ 6 5 4
  ◇ 6 5          W       E        ◇ J 4 3 2
  ♣ Q 10 4 2          S           ♣ K 8
                ♠ Q 5 4 2
                ♡ A K 7 3
                ◇ Q
                ♣ A J 7 6
```

West leads the queen of hearts from his strong sequence, and your
first problem is whether to capture this trick or hold up. On the whole
it is better to win, because a spade switch could be awkward; you would
have to play low from dummy and East might be able to win and shift to
clubs.

You win the first heart, therefore, and lead the queen of diamonds, on
which West play low. This is the critical moment. If you fail to overtake,
you have to use the ace of spades to enter dummy, and then, if the jack of
diamonds does not fall under the A K, you will not be able to bring in
the rest of the suit.

Since five diamonds will be enough for your contract you make the
safety play of overtaking the queen with the king. Then you force out the
jack and the ace of spades is still there as an entry.

37

Example 21

The next hand has the same general theme: the declarer makes an unusual play to preserve the entry for a long suit. But this time it is done not by overtaking a high card, but by refusing to part with an entry, at the cost of an obvious trick.

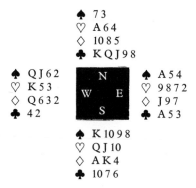

```
                    ♠ 7 3
                    ♡ A 6 4
                    ◇ 10 8 5
                    ♣ K Q J 9 8
      ♠ Q J 6 2       N         ♠ A 5 4
      ♡ K 5 3      W     E      ♡ 9 8 7 2
      ◇ Q 6 3 2                 ◇ J 9 7
      ♣ 4 2            S        ♣ A 5 3
                    ♠ K 10 9 8
                    ♡ Q J 10
                    ◇ A K 4
                    ♣ 10 7 6
```

North opened with a sub-standard one club, justified perhaps by the good suit, and South responded three no trumps, which was passed out. West led the two of spades and East won with the ace.

After some thought East returned the nine of hearts. This was good play on his part. West's lead of the two of spades suggested a suit of four cards only, so there was little future there. More important was to drive out the ace of hearts, which would be an entry for the clubs, once this suit has been established.

South covered the nine of hearts with the ten and West played the king. This presented the declarer with the chance of making three tricks in hearts, but nevertheless he played low from dummy. West returned a heart, won by the jack. Now South set about the clubs. East won the third round and led a spade. South took the king, entered dummy with the ace of hearts, and cashed the remaining clubs. Thus he made game with four clubs, two diamonds, two hearts and one spade.

It is clear that if South had parted with the ace of hearts on the first round of the suit, he would have had no entry for the long clubs.

Example 22

There is opportunity sometimes to make two safety plays in the same suit. A card that would be wrong on the first round becomes right on the second round. Observe South's management of the spade suit on the following deal:

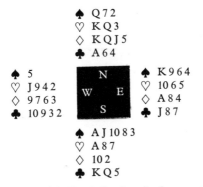

♠ Q72
♡ KQ3
◇ KQJ5
♣ A64

♠ 5
♡ J942
◇ 9763
♣ 10932

N W E S

♠ K964
♡ 1065
◇ A84
♣ J87

♠ AJ1083
♡ A87
◇ 102
♣ KQ5

Bidding with plenty of spirit, North-South arrived at a contract of six spades. West led the two of clubs and declarer was in dummy. As the ace of diamonds was a certain loser, it was clear that South needed to pick up the trump suit without loss.

As declarer, would you begin with a low spade from dummy or with the queen? On the present hand it would make no difference, but in some cases the queen would be a mistake. Suppose that East held the singleton king; then a lead of the queen would establish a trick for West's 9 x x x.

Following the general principle, therefore, of leading low for a finesse unless a solid sequence is held, South began with the two of spades from dummy. West played the four and the jack held the trick. South then entered dummy with a heart for a second lead of spades.

Whereas the queen would have been a mistake on the first round, now it is correct. East will probably cover with the king; then South crosses to dummy again in hearts and finesses against East's 9 x of spades.

If declarer leads the seven of spades from dummy on the second round he can hardly let it run without second sight. He puts in the ten from hand, but then East's K 9 wins a certain trick.

Examples 23 and 24

On many hands safety consists of losing the lead (if at all) to one opponent rather than the other. The two deals that follow illustrate that point.

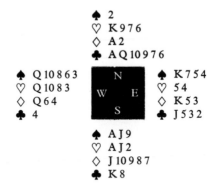

You are South, playing in three no trumps. West leads the six of spades and East plays the king. As you have a chance of second trick with the J 9, you win with the ace.

Counting your tricks, you see that you have four certain winners outside the clubs. Thus five tricks in clubs will be enough for game. The only danger lies in a spade lead from East through your J 9.

To avert this danger you decide to establish the clubs without giving East a chance to gain the lead. You cross to dummy with the king of hearts and lead a low club. When East plays low, you put in the eight. As it happens, the eight holds the trick. You then cash the king, cross to the ace of diamonds, and run the rest of the clubs.

You would not have minded if the eight of clubs had lost to the jack in West's hand, because no attack by West would cause you any problem. If he switched to diamonds, for example, you would go up with the ace and lead the ace of clubs, dropping your king beneath it.

In the last example your unusual play of the club suit was caused by the vulnerable holding in spades. On the next hand there is a question of timing. It is not safe to allow East to win the first trick, because he may probe a weak spot in another suit.

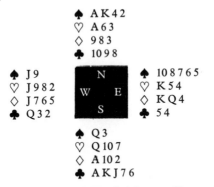

```
                    ♠ A K 4 2
                    ♡ A 6 3
                    ◇ 9 8 3
                    ♣ 10 9 8
    ♠ J 9              N          ♠ 10 8 7 6 5
    ♡ J 9 8 2      W     E        ♡ K 5 4
    ◇ J 7 6 5                     ◇ K Q 4
    ♣ Q 3 2          S            ♣ 5 4
                    ♠ Q 3
                    ♡ Q 10 7
                    ◇ A 10 2
                    ♣ A K J 7 6
```

South was in three no trumps and West led the two of hearts. Declarer could be sure of two tricks in hearts by playing low from dummy, but he realized there was a danger in this line; East might be able to win with the king of hearts and switch to diamonds.

South made the excellent play, therefore, of going up with the ace of hearts and finessing the ten of clubs. West won this trick and switched to diamonds, but the game was safe now. South won the first diamond to avoid the danger of a lead through his Q 10 of hearts. He had nine sure tricks by way of four clubs, three spades, and two red aces.

If declarer had played low from dummy on the first round of hearts, East would have won with the king and might well have switched to the king of diamonds. South can make the contract if he does everything right (he must take the second diamond, then play three rounds of spades, giving West an awkward discard), but in practice he would probably take the club finesse sooner or later.

Example 25

An ace will (usually) win a trick and will sometimes furnish an invaluable discard. If these two functions can be combined, the profit will be the greater.

The following hand was played in a pairs event before the stratagem used by the declarer was as well known as it is to-day.

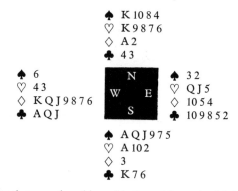

♠ K 10 8 4
♡ K 9 8 7 6
◇ A 2
♣ 4 3

♠ 6
♡ 4 3
◇ K Q J 9 8 7 6
♣ A Q J

♠ 3 2
♡ Q J 5
◇ 10 5 4
♣ 10 9 8 5 2

♠ A Q J 9 7 5
♡ A 10 2
◇ 3
♣ K 7 6

North-South were vulnerable, and in face of determined defence by West they went to five spades over five diamonds. All passed and West made the normal lead of the king of diamonds.

South would have enough tricks if he could establish the hearts, but in doing this he might lose the lead to East, who would hasten to play a club through the king. A reasonable plan for declarer would be to win with the ace of diamonds, draw trumps, and lead a low heart from the table, hoping to duck the trick into West's hand. This line fails because East has both queen and jack of hearts and will no doubt play one of them when the low card is led from dummy.

South can improve his chances considerably by the clever play of ducking the first round of diamonds. If West continues diamonds, he discards a heart from hand, draws trumps, then plays off ace and king of hearts. When all follow, he ruffs the third round (remember he has disposed of a heart on the ace of diamonds), returns to dummy with a trump, and makes two more heart tricks, discarding clubs from hand. He loses just one diamond and one club.

Example 26

Many forms of safety play are directed towards retaining control in a suit contract. Every player knows that it can be disastrous to arrive at a point where a defender has more trumps than the declarer. The following hand illustrates one way of avoiding that situation.

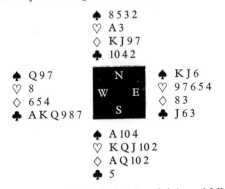

South is in four hearts. West leads the king of clubs and follows with the ace.

The contract (so long as you haven't looked at the opposing hands) seems safe enough. Why not ruff, draw the trumps, and run the diamonds, making nine tricks in the red suits plus the ace of spades ?

See what happens if declarer follows that line. West shows out on the second trump, and when declarer turns to diamonds (better than drawing two more trumps) East ruffs the third round and plays another club. After South has ruffed this, East has yet another trump trick to come, plus two tricks in spades.

The safe play, guarding against five trumps in one hand, is to discard losing spades on the second and third rounds of clubs. If West leads yet a fourth club, South ruffs low in dummy and has no difficulty in making the rest of the tricks.

Example 27

The same sort of problem arises on the next hand, but now there are more complications in the play.

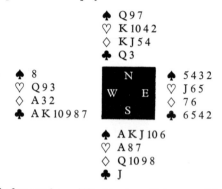

South is in four spades and West begins with two top clubs. Let us suppose that South ruffs and draws two rounds of trumps, discovering West's singleton. He can draw the rest of the trumps all right, but it will take all his own trumps to do so, and he still has not forced out the ace of diamonds.

The best plan, therefore, after two rounds of trumps, would be to switch to diamonds. If West could be persuaded to part with his ace of diamonds on the first round, declarer's problems would be over, as dummy could take care of any future club lead. But a good player in West's position would hold up the ace of diamonds on the first round. He would win the second round and give his partner a ruff. East would exit with his last trump, and South would eventually lose a fourth trick in hearts.

These troubles are avoided if South, recognizing that his control of the trump situation is open to attack, declines to ruff the second club, discarding a heart. It is true that there is a slight risk that the diamonds may be 4—1 and that the defenders will take an immediate ruff, but the danger of that is much less than of losing trump control. (If West had held a low singleton in diamonds he might well have led it, and if he has A x x x he may not find the switch.)

Examples 28, 29 and 30

In the last two examples the declarer declined to ruff in his own hand, so that the dummy could eventually take care of the dangerous suit. The same purpose can be achieved by giving up a trump trick early on when there is a likely, or even possible, loser in the trump suit. Then, as before, dummy can take the force and declarer does not weaken his own trump length. The three examples below are all examples of this type of play; after studying them, you will not fail to recognize similar hands at the table.

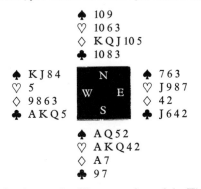

```
                ♠  10 9
                ♡  10 6 3
                ◇  K Q J 10 5
                ♣  10 8 3
  ♠  K J 8 4                      ♠  7 6 3
  ♡  5              N             ♡  J 9 8 7
  ◇  9 8 6 3      W   E           ◇  4 2
  ♣  A K Q 5         S            ♣  J 6 4 2
                ♠  A Q 5 2
                ♡  A K Q 4 2
                ◇  A 7
                ♣  9 7
```

South plays in four hearts after West opened one club. The defence begins with three rounds of clubs. Suppose that South ruffs and draws two rounds of trumps, discovering West's singleton. He cannot force out East's winning trump, because East will then make the setting trick in clubs; and the spade finesse is likely to be wrong because West has opened the bidding.

South's best chance is to test the diamonds, hoping that East will follow to four rounds; but alas, East ruffs the third round and exits with a trump. The contract will now be defeated by two tricks.

It would not help South on this occasion to refuse to ruff the third club. Having ruffed the club, he should reflect that he can afford to lose a trick in hearts, and he must aim to lose it while there is still a trump in dummy. So he plays off ace of hearts and follows with a *low* one. East wins and cannot effectively play a club because there is still a trump in dummy. East will probably exit with a spade. South goes up with the ace, draws the remaining trumps, and runs his five diamond tricks without any unseemly interruption.

Having studied that hand, you won't go wrong on the next one:

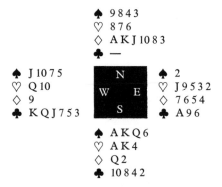

```
                    ♠ 9 8 4 3
                    ♡ 8 7 6
                    ◇ A K J 10 8 3
                    ♣ —
    ♠ J 10 7 5          N          ♠ 2
    ♡ Q 10                         ♡ J 9 5 3 2
    ◇ 9          W         E       ◇ 7 6 5 4
    ♣ K Q J 7 5 3        S         ♣ A 9 6
                    ♠ A K Q 6
                    ♡ A K 4
                    ◇ Q 2
                    ♣ 10 8 4 2
```

West leads the king of clubs against six spades. Declarer ruffs in dummy and plays a spade to the ace, to which all follow. If he plays another high trump, the contract disappears out of the window. Dummy at this stage will have only one trump left, South will hold Q 6 and West J 10. South may ruff a club and turn to diamonds, but West will ruff the second round and cash two more club tricks, with a heart to follow at the finish.

South should give up his trump trick on the second, or even the first round. Then there will still be a trump in dummy to take care of a club from West. Contract made instead of down three!

The third hand is similar, but perhaps a little more difficult because now it is essential to make the safety play on the very first round of trumps.

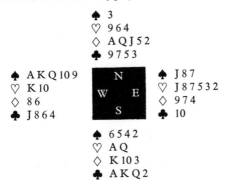

```
                    ♠ 3
                    ♡ 9 6 4
                    ◇ A Q J 5 2
                    ♣ 9 7 5 3
    ♠ A K Q 10 9                    ♠ J 8 7
    ♡ K 10          N               ♡ J 8 7 5 3 2
    ◇ 8 6        W     E            ◇ 9 7 4
    ♣ J 8 6 4       S               ♣ 10
                    ♠ 6 5 4 2
                    ♡ A Q
                    ◇ K 10 3
                    ♣ A K Q 2
```

North-South did well to finish in five clubs, the only game contract that had a chance. West won the first trick with the king of spades, and after some consideration led a diamond to the second trick. If South had held only two diamonds, this would have been a fine defence, as a second diamond would cut the declarer away from dummy's suit.

As it was, South won the diamond switch with the king, ruffed a spade, and led a trump from dummy. East played the ten and was allowed to hold the trick! Now everything was under control. South won the heart return, ruffed another spade, drew trumps, and ran off the diamonds, making game with three top trumps, two ruffs, ace of hearts, and five diamonds.

Let us see what would have happened if South had ducked the second round of clubs instead of the first. West would have won and promptly returned a trump, removing the last club from dummy (South has already ruffed a spade, remember). That would have left South one trick short. He needed two spade ruffs, and the only safe way to negotiate them was to ruff a spade at the first opportunity, then give up the first round of trumps.

Example 31

One of the commonest forms of play consists of taking a ruff in the short trump hand, thus increasing the number of tricks that can be won in the trump suit. In this area, too, various safety plays can be employed to increase the chance of a ruff. Two of them appear in the following hand from a pairs event.

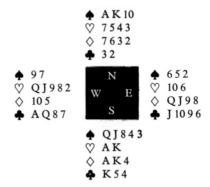

```
              ♠ A K 10
              ♡ 7 5 4 3
              ◇ 7 6 3 2
              ♣ 3 2
  ♠ 9 7              N         ♠ 6 5 2
  ♡ Q J 9 8 2                  ♡ 10 6
  ◇ 10 5      W         E      ◇ Q J 9 8
  ♣ A Q 8 7          S         ♣ J 10 9 6
              ♠ Q J 8 4 3
              ♡ A K
              ◇ A K 4
              ♣ K 5 4
```

The best contract for North-South is three no trumps, but a number of pairs finished in four spades. The usual lead against four spades was the queen of hearts, won by the declarer's ace.

Counting his tricks in a spade contract, South can see five in the trump suit plus two A K's. There is an excellent chance to establish a tenth trick by ruffing the third round of clubs, and the cautious declarers set about this at once by leading a club from hand at trick two. Whatever the return, declarer played another round of clubs and could not be prevented from ruffing the third round.

Nevertheless, some players were defeated in four spades. After winning the first heart they crossed to dummy with a trump and optimistically led a club towards the king. West took the ace and promptly switched to trumps. As one round of trumps had been played already, the result was that South was unable to ruff any club at all, for naturally East won the next round of clubs and knocked out the third trump!

At one table the declarer had to contend with an opening lead of trumps. This appears to ruin his hopes of club ruff, but he still made the contract by cleverly taking advantage of a genuine 'half chance'.

In dummy at trick one South led a club, on which East played the jack. If the king of clubs was over the ace, it would provide a tenth trick anyway, so for the moment South played low. East followed his partner's defence by returning a trump to dummy. When East played the ten on the next round of clubs, South covered with the king, forcing West to take the trick. Luck was with him, as West had no more trumps to lead. Thus South was able to develop his tenth trick by ruffing the third club in dummy.

Example 32

We have seen in previous examples that many safety plays are designed to retain communication between the two hands; often a trick that could easily be won is surrendered for this purpose.

The deal below shows a slightly different situation: a trick is surrendered, not to retain an entry card, but to create one.

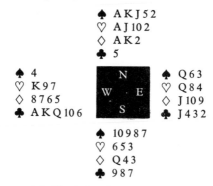

```
                    ♠ A K J 5 2
                    ♡ A J 10 2
                    ◇ A K 2
                    ♣ 5
    ♠ 4                                ♠ Q 6 3
    ♡ K 9 7         N                  ♡ Q 8 4
    ◇ 8 7 6 5     W     E              ◇ J 10 9
    ♣ A K Q 10 6    S                  ♣ J 4 3 2
                    ♠ 10 9 8 7
                    ♡ 6 5 3
                    ◇ Q 4 3
                    ♣ 9 8 7
```

West opens one club, North doubles, and after a pass by East South responds one spade. North raises to four spades and all pass. West leads the king of clubs and follows with a second club, forcing dummy to ruff.

It may seem that the natural play is to lead out ace and king of spades. If the queen falls, South will have enough entries to hand to finesse hearts twice. If, at worst, the ace and king of spades do not bring down the queen, declarer can try leading the jack of hearts from dummy; this will be good enough if West has K Q x, because South will later come to hand with the queen of diamonds and pick up the rest of the heart suit by a finesse.

It can be seen that as the cards lie this play will not succeed. After ace and king of spades declarer leads the jack of hearts from dummy, losing to West's king; when the heart finesse is taken later, it loses to the queen.

So, what can be done? The answer is that, lacking entries to hand, but able to afford the loss of one trump trick, South should play off ace of spades at trick three and then follow with the *jack* of spades. East makes his queen and, we will say, exits with a club. South is careful to ruff this with a high trump in dummy; then he draws the outstanding trump with the ten and leads a heart, finessing the jack and losing to the queen. He will regain the lead later with the queen of diamonds, and a second finesse of hearts will win the contract.

You will find it useful to play this hand over two or three times, for it contains a valuable lesson in the care and management of entries.

Example 33

In any no trump contract it is normal and necessary for the declarer to pay special attention to the suit led. He should ask himself in particular: 'How many cards does the leader hold? What are the dangers in this suit and how can they be met?'

Here is an example of a contract thrown away because the declarer failed to make these calculations:

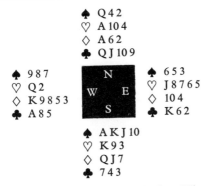

South was in three no trumps and West led the five of diamonds. The two was played from dummy and the ten by East. South won and . . .

You're right! Natural as it seemed to head the ten with the queen, it was the wrong play here, as the sequel soon showed. Aware, perhaps, that he had already made a mistake, South tried to recover by crossing to dummy with a spade and leading the nine of clubs from the table. East did very well to put on the king, thus protecting his partner's entry. Now a diamond was led through South's J 7. Declarer won the third round in dummy, but his fears were confirmed when West won the next club and defeated the contract with two more diamond tricks.

The main danger to this contract was that West might hold five diamonds and one of the club honours. Suppose that South plays low on the first lead (as no doubt he would have done had he held K x x instead of Q J x). East leads a second diamond, but when he comes in with the king of clubs he cannot clear the suit.

It is true that playing the queen of diamonds on the first trick would be right if West held both ace and king of clubs; but that, obviously, is against the odds.

Example 34

On many hands played in a suit contract the declarer has to choose whether to play a 'ruffing game', planning to ruff losers in dummy, or to play for 'suit establishment'—drawing trumps and then running a long suit. Which course is better cannot be judged in advance of individual circumstances, but this much can be said in advance: when the choice appears to be close, the suit establishment game tends to be better, because the declarer has more chances to overcome a bad trump division.

The following hand is a typical example:

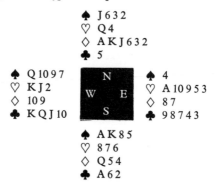

```
              ♠ J 6 3 2
              ♡ Q 4
              ◇ A K J 6 3 2
              ♣ 5
  ♠ Q 10 9 7          ♠ 4
  ♡ K J 2      N      ♡ A 10 9 5 3
  ◇ 10 9    W   E     ◇ 8 7
  ♣ K Q J 10    S     ♣ 9 8 7 4 3
              ♠ A K 8 5
              ♡ 8 7 6
              ◇ Q 5 4
              ♣ A 6 2
```

South is in four spades and West leads the king of clubs. It is interesting to consider how players of three different grades would tackle this problem.

That legendary character, Mrs Guggenheim, who could never resist 'ruffing in', would win with the ace of clubs and hastily ruff a club. Returning to hand with the ace of spades, she would ruff another club, then play dummy's last spade to the king. Now, even if the trumps were 3—2, she would be in difficulties, having three heart losers: she would need, in effect, the hand with the outstanding trump to hold at least three diamonds.

A better player would not dream of weakening the dummy by ruffing. He (or she) would win the club lead and play off ace and king of spades, then play on diamonds, making the contract very easily whenever the spades were 3—2. But on the present occasion that line would fail. If South followed with a third spade, West would go up with the queen and play a club, forcing dummy to ruff with the jack of spades and establishing a trick for his ten. Alternatively, South might turn to diamonds after two rounds of trumps; then West would ruff the third diamond, cash the queen of spades, and take two tricks in hearts.

Finally, an expert in safety manoeuvres would recognize that the contract could be made not only when trumps were 3—2, but also when West held Q 10 x x. He would play ace of spades, then a low spade. West cannot do better than go up with the queen, take two hearts, then exit with a club, which dummy ruffs. Now declarer cashes the jack of spades, returns to hand with the queen of diamonds to draw the outstanding trump, and discards his remaining losers on dummy's diamond suit.

Example 35

Some players, like Mrs Guggenheim in the preceding example, are very fond of making low trumps by ruffing; others have a strong fancy for finesses, whose successful accomplishment seems to give them a feeling of superiority. On the following deal both tendencies had to be resisted, for better safety. It occurred in a mixed pairs event and was excellently handled by the partner of one of the authors.

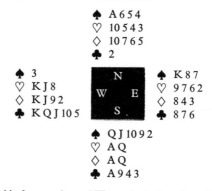

```
                    ♠ A 6 5 4
                    ♡ 10 5 4 3
                    ◊ 10 7 6 5
                    ♣ 2
    ♠ 3                           ♠ K 8 7
    ♡ K J 8            N          ♡ 9 7 6 2
    ◊ K J 9 2      W     E        ◊ 8 4 3
    ♣ K Q J 10 5       S          ♣ 8 7 6
                    ♠ Q J 10 9 2
                    ♡ A Q
                    ◊ A Q
                    ♣ A 9 4 3
```

South played in four spades and West, who had made a take-out double of the opening one spade, led the king of clubs.

Three finesses were offered, but South took none of them! This was her line of play:

Win with ace of clubs, ruff a club with a low trump; return to ace of hearts, ruff another club low; return to ace of diamonds, ruff the next club with the ace of spades; lead a spade and lose just the three kings.

You may think that it would not have been particularly dangerous to finesse in one of the red suits, but observe the consequence of doing that. West wins and promptly leads his singleton trump. South may go up with dummy's ace, but when she tries to ruff the fourth round of clubs she is overruffed by East's eight of spades. The only safe line was the one she followed.

Example 36

We saw several hands earlier on where the declarer refused to ruff in his own hand in order to protect his length in trumps. Occasionally a rather different situation occurs: declarer refuses to ruff in dummy, the hand with the shorter trumps, so as to retain an entry for dummy's side suit. Here is an example of this comparatively rare situation:

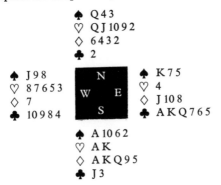

```
              ♠ Q43
              ♡ QJ1092
              ◇ 6432
              ♣ 2
  ♠ J98          N        ♠ K75
  ♡ 87653     W     E     ♡ 4
  ◇ 7                      ◇ J108
  ♣ 10984        S        ♣ AKQ765
              ♠ A1062
              ♡ AK
              ◇ AKQ95
              ♣ J3
```

South played in five diamonds after East had overcalled in clubs. West led the ten of clubs, won by East's queen. Most players in East's position would be attracted by the singleton heart, but East was sure that South held the ace of hearts and played the stronger defence of leading a second club, with a view to forcing the dummy. South ruffed and drew two rounds of trumps, but from that point of trumps, but from that point the hand went sour. He drew the third trump, cashed ace and king of hearts, then led a low spade to the queen and king. East returned a spade and another trick had to be lost.

Despite the excellent defence, South could have made his contract by a clever counterstroke. Instead of ruffing the second club, he discards a spade from dummy. If East plays a third club, South ruffs with the nine, draws trumps, cashes the top hearts, and enters dummy by leading the five of diamonds to dummy's six.

Example 37

Nobody who was investing his capital would be satisfied with the possibility of a 10% return on his money when there was a chance of losing the entire amount.

Similarly, at bridge, it is silly to risk any contract, and particularly a slam contract, for the sake of a possible overtrick (worth a good deal less than 10% of the amount at stake).

One of the authors was partnered at rubber bridge by a player who was in the habit of 'shaving an egg' when he played bridge: he would always capture a trick with the smallest card available, despite the risk of blocking a suit or being unable to give his partner the lead. The rubber on this occasion went very well for a while, but all good things come to an end.

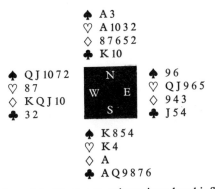

```
              ♠ A 3
              ♡ A 10 3 2
              ◇ 8 7 6 5 2
              ♣ K 10

♠ Q J 10 7 2              ♠ 9 6
♡ 8 7           N         ♡ Q J 9 6 5
◇ K Q J 10    W   E       ◇ 9 4 3
♣ 3 2           S         ♣ J 5 4

              ♠ K 8 5 4
              ♡ K 4
              ◇ A
              ♣ A Q 9 8 7 6
```

South opened one club; North, not caring to introduce his flimsy diamond suit, responded one heart; and South rebid three clubs. This, perhaps, was not quite in the modern style—one spade would be more fashionable—but it was a fair expression of South's values. North now jumped to six clubs, expecting this contract to present no difficulty.

West led the king of diamonds against six clubs. South judged correctly that the best plan would be to ruff two spades in dummy. He began with a spade to the ace, led back a spade to the king, then played a third round, ruffing with dummy's ten of clubs. East overruffed with the jack and returned a trump to dummy's king. Now there was no parking-place for the fourth spade.

This was a scandalous disregard of the safety regulations! The contract could hardly fail once two rounds of spades had gone by safely. The next play should be a spade, ruffed by the *king*, a diamond ruff, and a fourth spade, ruffed by the ten. East can overruff, but that is the only trick for the defence.

Always watch out for situations where a high ruff is safer than a low ruff.

Examples 38 and 39

One of the commonest and most useful manoeuvres in defence is the refusal to overruff the declarer in a situation such as this:

```
              5 2
K 10 4               8 3
           A Q J 9 7 6
```

This is the trump suit and at some point in the play East leads a suit of which both declarer and West are void. South ruffs with the queen, and West, by declining to overruff, ensures a second trump trick for his side.

The same type of play is available to the declarer. Consider this deal:

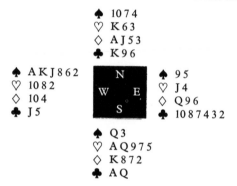

```
              ♠ 10 7 4
              ♡ K 6 3
              ◇ A J 5 3
              ♣ K 9 6

♠ A K J 8 6 2           ♠ 9 5
♡ 10 8 2                ♡ J 4
◇ 10 4                  ◇ Q 9 6
♣ J 5                   ♣ 10 8 7 4 3 2

              ♠ Q 3
              ♡ A Q 9 7 5
              ◇ K 8 7 2
              ♣ A Q
```

South plays in four hearts and West, who has overcalled in spades, begins with king, ace and jack of this suit. Although the jack of spades is a master, East very properly ruffs with the jack of hearts and South overruffs with the queen. When he follows with the king and ace of hearts he is disappointed to find that the ten is still out against him. He can throw one diamond on the king of clubs, but sooner or later has to lose a trump and a diamond.

South made his mistake when he overruffed the jack of hearts. Instead, he should have discarded a diamond. Then he has no problem in drawing the trumps, cashing ace and queen of clubs, and discarding his other diamond loser on the king of clubs.

In a second example the hand that is shorter in trumps must discard a loser instead of overruffing.

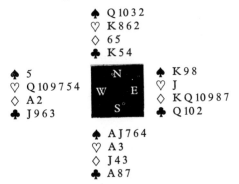

```
              ♠ Q 10 3 2
              ♡ K 8 6 2
              ◇ 6 5
              ♣ K 5 4
  ♠ 5                        ♠ K 9 8
  ♡ Q 10 9 7 5 4      N      ♡ J
  ◇ A 2          W       E   ◇ K Q 10 9 8 7
  ♣ J 9 6 3          S       ♣ Q 10 2
              ♠ A J 7 6 4
              ♡ A 3
              ◇ J 4 3
              ♣ A 8 7
```

South plays in four spades after East has overcalled in diamonds. West leads the ace of diamonds and continues with the two to his partner's queen.

East is shrewd enough to realize (1) that his partner has no more diamonds, and (2) that if his partner can contribute a trump on the third round, he will force the ten of spades from dummy and establish a trick for the K 9 8. With this idea in mind, he returns the king of diamonds and West gallantly puts in his five of trumps.

It does not look bad to overruff—but if declarer does so, he will lose a trump trick to East and a club trick later on.

The right game is to discard the losing club from dummy instead of overruffing. Then the king of trumps can be picked up by a finesse and the third round of clubs can be ruffed on the table.

Example 40

We conclude this little study of safety plays with two coups that were considered the height of brilliancy when they were first described. (It would be pleasant, though somewhat naive, to suppose that they had their birth at the table rather than in the mind of an analyst.) By now, these plays are well understood, and once the idea is familiar they are not difficult to execute.

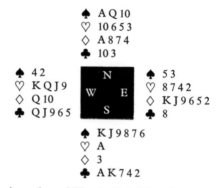

```
              ♠ A Q 10
              ♡ 10 6 5 3
              ◇ A 8 7 4
              ♣ 10 3
  ♠ 4 2          N          ♠ 5 3
  ♡ K Q J 9   W     E       ♡ 8 7 4 2
  ◇ Q 10         S          ◇ K J 9 6 5 2
  ♣ Q J 9 6 5               ♣ 8
              ♠ K J 9 8 7 6
              ♡ A
              ◇ 3
              ♣ A K 7 4 2
```

South plays in six spades and West leads the king of hearts. Obviously the clubs have to be developed, so declarer wins the heart and at once plays off ace and king of clubs. Bang! East ruffs and returns a trump. South suddenly finds that he has only two trumps in dummy and has three losers to ruff. It can't be done.

The safety play is to cash only one high club and to follow with a *low* club. The defenders take this and play a trump, but with K x x of clubs remaining, and still two trumps in dummy, declarer can comfortably ruff his two losers.

What would happen, do you think, if West were to strike a trump lead ?

Now ace and another club is not good enough, as West will win and play a second trump, leaving South with two club losers and only one spade in dummy.

However, as the cards lie, South can overcome the trump lead in another way. He cashes the ace of clubs, crosses to the ace of diamonds, and leads a second club from dummy. If East ruffs, he has no more trumps to lead; and if East lets this trick go, South wins and ruffs two clubs, losing the last one only.

Note the play of leading the second club *towards* the king, so that if East ruffs he will be ruffing a loser. It is an example of 'avoidance play' and is one of the commonest forms of safety play.

Example 41

Our final example is perhaps more a 'communication play' than a safety play. However, since it increases the declarer's chances by about 50%, it is a safety play in that sense.

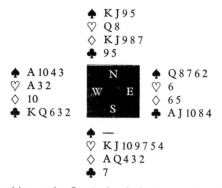

```
              ♠ K J 9 5
              ♡ Q 8
              ◇ K J 9 8 7
              ♣ 9 5
  ♠ A 10 4 3       N        ♠ Q 8 7 6 2
  ♡ A 3 2      W       E    ♡ 6
  ◇ 10                      ◇ 6 5
  ♣ K Q 6 3 2      S        ♣ A J 10 8 4
              ♠ —
              ♡ K J 10 9 7 5 4
              ◇ A Q 4 3 2
              ♣ 7
```

After a competitive auction South plays in five hearts. West leads his singleton diamond, hoping to come in with the ace of hearts and give his partner the lead in either spades or clubs.

From declarer's point of view, the danger is obvious. The lead is surely a singleton, the ace of trumps has to be forced out, and the opponents can go from hand to hand in clubs.

Suppose South makes the obvious play of a trump at trick two. West will win and lead a club to his partner's ace. East, taking his cue from the fact that West has led a diamond rather than a suit bid by his side, will return a diamond for West to ruff.

Can declarer avert this sequence of plays ? Yes, by the brilliant stroke of leading the king of spades from dummy at trick two. He intends, if this is not covered by the ace, to discard his losing club. In that way he exchanges a club loser for a spade loser and meanwhile cuts the communications between the defending hands. The play is called the 'Scissors Coup'.

In this account of safety plays we have not aimed to present difficult or spectacular coups, but problems of a type you will meet often and will readily recognize. Note that to execute these plays it is not necessary to reconstruct or count the adverse hands, as is required for most forms of end-play.

When you have read and re-read the example hands, you will have learned to foresee the danger of bad distribution. You may meet slightly different problems at the table, but you will have mastered certain principles and will be able to apply them to a variety of new situations.